SECOND EDITION

WHAT TO DO WHEN YOU WORRY TOO MUCH

A Kid's Guide to OVERCOMING ANXIETY

by **Dawn Huebner, PhD**

illustrated by
Sabine Rothmund

Magination Press • Washington, DC
American Psychological Association

NOTES ON THE SECOND EDITION

The original *What to Do When You Worry Too Much* was published in 2005, filling a critical need in the literature. Warm, empowering, and wholly original, it rocketed to the top of sales charts, where it has remained for close to 20 years. So, why revise it? Well, times have changed, and with them, our understanding of anxiety. The challenge, then, was to keep the best parts of *What to Do When You Worry Too Much*—the conversational tone, interactive elements, clear and actionable strategies—while updating the content to reflect best practices. That's what you will find here. A book that is both familiar and new. The beloved *What to Do When You Worry Too Much* made better.

For those who worry too much: I see you. I believe in you—*DH*

For my sister, Julia—*SR*

Magination Press
Books for Kids From the
American Psychological Association

Magination Press is a registered trademark of the American Psychological Association. Order books at maginationpress.org or call 1-800-374-2721.

Book design by Christina Gaugler
Printed by Sheridan Worzalla, Stevens Point, WI

Library of Congress Cataloging-in-Publication Data

Names: Huebner, Dawn, author. | Rothmund, Sabine, illustrator.
Title: What to do when you worry too much : a kid's guide to overcoming anxiety / by Dawn Huebner, PhD ; illustrated by Sabine Rothmund.
Description: Second edition. | Washington, D.C. : Magination Press, [2025] | Series: What-to-do guides for kids series | Summary: "Second edition, guides children and parents through the cognitive-behavioral techniques most often used in the treatment of anxiety"— Provided by publisher.
Identifiers: LCCN 2024007784 (print) | LCCN 2024007785 (ebook) | ISBN 9781433844881 (paperback) | ISBN 9781433844898 (ebook)
Subjects: LCSH: Worry in children—Juvenile literature. | Anxiety in children—Juvenile literature. | BISAC: JUVENILE NONFICTION / Health & Daily Living / Mental Health | JUVENILE NONFICTION / Social Topics / Self-Esteem & Self-Reliance
Classification: LCC BF723.W67 H84 2025 (print) | LCC BF723.W67 (ebook) | DDC 155.4/1246—dc23/eng/20240318
LC record available at https://lccn.loc.gov/2024007784
LC ebook record available at https://lccn.loc.gov/2024007785

Manufactured in the United States of America

10 9 8 7 6 5 4 3 2 1

TABLE OF CONTENTS

Note to Parents and Caregivers • 4

CHAPTER 1   **Are You Growing Worries? • 7**

CHAPTER 2   **What Is a Worry? • 13**

CHAPTER 3   **How Do Worries Get Started? • 19**

CHAPTER 4   **Quieting the Alarm • 25**

CHAPTER 5   **Using Logic • 37**

CHAPTER 6   **Talking Back to Worry • 47**

CHAPTER 7   **Doing the Opposite • 53**

CHAPTER 8   **Spending Less Time With Worry • 59**

CHAPTER 9   **Staying Healthy and Strong • 71**

CHAPTER 10   **You Can Do It! • 77**

About the Author, Illustrator, and Magination Press • 80

NOTE TO PARENTS AND CAREGIVERS

If you are the parent or caregiver of an anxious child, you know what it's like to be held captive by fear. So does your child. Children who worry too much go to great lengths to avoid frightening situations, unable to shake the fear of what *might* happen. Unfortunately, the more children capitulate to anxiety, the more powerful it becomes. You have undoubtedly seen this pattern and done your best to reverse it, reassuring, distracting, accommodating, and/or encouraging your child, but it doesn't work. None of it. At least, not in the long run. Anxiety can be neither forced nor jollied away.

But there is hope.

What to Do When You Worry Too Much, Second Edition, teaches a new way of thinking about and managing anxiety, one that addresses fear where it begins: in the brain. Your child's brain is alert to potential threat, broadly defined as anything that could hurt, embarrass, lead to uncertainty, or cause unpleasant feelings. Threat triggers an alarm, which makes it feel like the danger is real. Your child tries to protect themselves. Who wouldn't? You, as an adult, know that the danger isn't real, which puts the ball in your court. What should you do?

If you tell your child that they are safe and push them to move forward, they feel unheard, which increases their sense of threat. If you allow them to avoid what they are afraid of, they assume that you agree, that the danger really is real and cannot be managed. It's a Catch-22.

Fortunately, there is a middle path, one that allows you to emotionally support your anxious child without accommodating their anxiety. The middle path begins with teaching your child about what is happening in their brain, and how to quiet their internal alarm. It continues with empathy, including a clear acknowledgement of how anxious your child feels. Next comes logic, during which you and your child will examine evidence and think about likelihood. It might be tempting to stop there, but that would be a mistake. To effect lasting change, you need to help your child externalize their anxiety, setting the stage for the most powerful strategies: talking back, doing the opposite, and setting a limit on worry.

What to Do When You Worry Too Much, Second Edition, teaches these cognitive-behavioral skills and more. Your child will benefit most if you work together. Sit comfortably. Read slowly, just one or two chapters at a time. Have your child look at the pictures and do the activities as directed. Help your child practice everything they are learning, first when they are calm, and eventually when they are anxious. Practice is what helps your child develop the brain pathways necessary for lasting change.

Change is likely to happen in fits and starts. That's normal. Re-read the book as needed. Maintain a calm and steady presence. Use humor. Be patient. Remember that even small steps tip the balance in your child's favor, helping them break free of Worry's hold.

There is often a genetic component to anxiety, which means that if you are the parent of an anxious child, you might be anxious, too. Perhaps you can join your child in using the strategies presented here; all work as well with adults as they do with children. If, however, you find yourself struggling to remain calm in the face of your child's feelings, or if anxiety is significantly interfering in your child's life, please seek support from a mental health professional.

Whether you are using this book on your own or in the context of therapy, maintain faith in your child's ability to take back control from Worry. Project an air of confidence. Anxiety is uncomfortable, but your child is not in danger. They are capable of responding differently, and so are you. Together, you can move toward the day when you will be able to say that your child *used* to worry too much, but not anymore. Won't that feel good?

CHAPTER 1

Are You Growing Worries?

Most things grow when you tend to them.

Have you ever planted a tomato seed?

If you cover your seed with soil, water it, and make sure it gets plenty of sunlight, a little green shoot will appear.

If you check the soil and add water when it is dry, the green shoot will turn into a stalk with leaves and flowers.

And then one day, a tomato will appear.

If you keep tending to your plant, more and more tomatoes will appear.

Soon you will have so many tomatoes you'll need to look up how to make tomato sauce and tomato soup.

Tomatoes will appear in your salad and next to your tuna fish.

You will find a tomato sandwich in your lunch bag and tomato juice for a snack.

Eventually, there will be so many tomatoes your mom or dad will suggest chopping them up to make tomato ice cream and tomato cookies!

All those tomatoes will have come from one little seed that you planted and tended every day.

Draw something you have helped to grow.

Did you know that worries are like tomatoes?

You can't eat them, but you can make them grow simply by paying attention to them.

Many children tend to their worries, even though they don't mean to. And then, what started as a little seed of worry turns into a huge pile of problems that they don't want but can't figure out how to get rid of.

If this has happened to you, if your worries have grown so big that they bother you almost every day, this book is for you.

The bad news, as you know, is that worries can grow quickly and cause a lot of trouble.

The good news, which you may not know, is that you have the power to keep worries from taking over. You do.

Keep reading and you will learn how.

CHAPTER 2

What Is a Worry?

There are lots of words for worry:

Whatever you call it, a worry is a thought that upsets you.

It can be a specific thought like,

What if my mom forgets to pick me up?

Or it can be more general, like the idea that something bad is going to happen, even though you aren't sure what the bad thing might be.

Everyone feels worried sometimes.

It's normal to feel worried on your way to the doctor if you think you might be getting a shot, or before a spelling test if the words are really hard.

Most kids worry at least a little if they are doing something for the first time, or if they have to walk into a dark room with no lights on at all.

Worries like that make sense.

Other worries make less sense, like thinking a monster is going to grab you, when monsters don't exist. Or worrying that no one likes you even though your classmates play with you every day.

Whether or not your worries make sense to other people, they sure feel real to you.

Draw or write about one of your worries.

When one of your worries first appears, you probably do what most people do.

You find someone to talk to.

If there's a problem, you try to solve it.

If it's a worry you've had before, you might try to distract yourself, or ask for a hug.

These are all good strategies, and often, they help.

But sometimes, they don't help. Even with hugs and reassurance, even with attempts to solve the problem, some worries stay stubbornly stuck.

If you are reading this book, you are probably a kid whose worries get stuck. You might have worries other people don't understand, or that last longer than people think they should.

Having trouble with worries is something you can be born with, just like you are born with a certain eye color or the ability to curl your tongue. Often children who worry a lot have a parent or some other relative who worries, too.

List the people you know who worry a lot.

People who don't understand worries often say, "Don't worry about that!"

If only it were that easy! But there is no magic wand to make worries disappear.

There is no magic wand, but there are things you can do to be less bothered. Things that can make even sticky worries go away.

The first step is understanding how worries get started.

CHAPTER 3

How Do Worries Get Started?

Life doesn't always go the way we want it to. Scary and upsetting things do sometimes happen. Seeing, hearing, or thinking about these things is one of the ways worries get started.

That's because we all have a special part in our brain called the amygdala (a-mig-da-la) which is always on the lookout for danger. When you see, hear, or think about scary and upsetting things, your amygdala sounds an alarm.

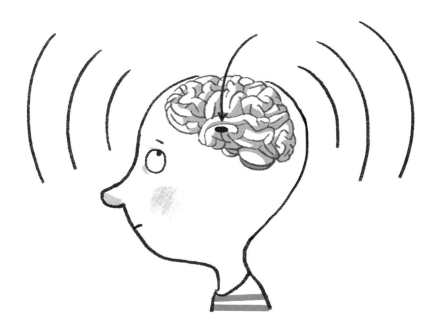

Just like the smoke detector on your ceiling, your amygdala is there to keep you safe.

Smoke detectors sound an alarm when there is smoke, because smoke might mean fire. But smoke doesn't always mean fire. It can also mean:

► A piece of toast is stuck in the toaster.

► Candles are burning.

► Food is sizzling on the stove.

A fire in your kitchen is an emergency. Food sizzling on the stove is not. Both set off the alarm, but running out of the house when your grilled cheese gets smokey doesn't solve anything.

Opening a window, turning on the fan, or lowering the heat under your food would be better things to do.

It's like that with your amygdala, too.

Your amygdala picks up on small cues that *might* mean danger, things that could hurt you, or embarrass you, or cause trouble for you.

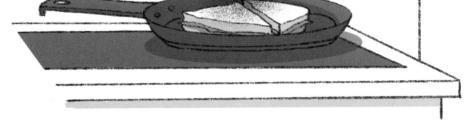

But what your brain is picking up on might not be an emergency, so immediately trying to escape might not be the right thing to do.

To choose the right response, you need to know if the danger is real. But it can be hard to know, because with both smoke detectors and brain alarms, it *feels* like the real thing every time. Even when it turns out to be a false alarm.

When your brain alarm goes off (for both real dangers and false alarms), your body gets ready to **RUN, FIGHT,** or **HIDE,** to protect yourself, in case the danger is real.

Your brain and body are doing exactly what they're supposed to do, but it doesn't feel very good. Your heart might be pounding. Your stomach might be churning. You might feel shaky or dizzy, like you are going to faint or throw up.

Lots of children have these uncomfortable feelings and don't realize it's their brain alarm that's causing them.

Put an X on the parts of your body you notice when your brain alarm goes off.

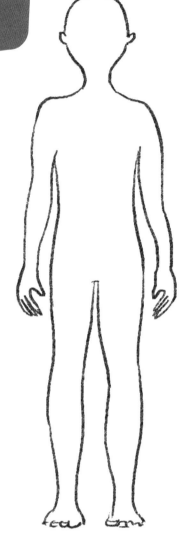

Circle the words that describe how you feel.

headache	sweaty	weak
tearful	tingly	nervous
nauseous	dizzy	scared
breathless	cold	unsure
heart racing	faint	worried
stomachache	shaky	angry

Brain alarms are impossible to ignore. And you shouldn't ignore them. But you also shouldn't assume that you are in **danger.**

Draw or write about a time your brain alarm went off and it turned out to be a false alarm.

No one wants to have false alarms. They aren't any fun, and they can cause other problems, too.

Brain alarms cause worry, and worry causes you to do things you wouldn't ordinarily do, like yell at people, or cry.

Worry makes you feel like you need to protect yourself by staying home or avoiding things other kids see as fun.

When the alarm goes off and worry kicks in, all you can think about is how to keep yourself safe.

Running away might be tempting, but it doesn't work. And it isn't the right solution. The right solution is to do something to quiet the alarm.

I don't want to!

CHAPTER 4

Quieting the Alarm

Whether or not the danger turns out to be real, brain alarms make it seem like the **WORST, MOST HORRIBLE THING** is about to happen. That's because when the alarm goes off, the thinking part of your brain shuts down.

Quieting the alarm turns the thinking part of your brain back on.

One of the best ways to quiet your brain alarm is to **breathe**.

Slowly and deeply.

On purpose.

Breathing slowly and deeply in the middle of an alarm is harder than it might seem. Your brain is telling you that something is wrong. Your body is gearing up to **RUN** or **FIGHT** or **HIDE**. You aren't in danger, but it feels like you are.

Stopping to take a few deep breaths is the last thing you are going to feel like doing, but it is exactly what your brain needs.

If you have a favorite breathing method, feel free to use it. If you don't already have a favorite, here's a method you can try:

Squeeze Tight Breaths

1. Take a deep breath in through your nose.

2. Hold it while you tense up all your muscles.

3. Squeeze your fists. Make your legs stiff like boards. Scrunch up your face.

4. Keep your body tight while you count to 5 in your head.

5. Breathe out through your mouth while you let all your muscles go loose.

6. Then do it again. And again. Three times in all.

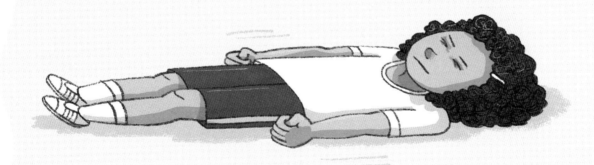

Mindfulness is another way to quiet your brain.

Mindfulness teaches you to pay attention to what is happening, to simply notice it, without trying to decide if it is good or bad. When you practice mindfulness, your brain learns to let go of unhelpful thoughts rather than grabbing onto and magnifying them.

Just like with breathing, there are lots of mindfulness activities. Here is one you can try.

Follow Your Senses

 Sit in a comfortable position.

Take a few breaths, in through your nose and out through your mouth.

Pay attention to each of your senses, and answer the following questions:

► What are 3 things you can see?

► What are 3 things you can hear?

► What are 3 things you can feel?

► What are 3 things you can smell?

► What are 3 things you can taste?

It will be easy to notice the first thing with each sense. The second thing might be harder, and the third thing harder still. Stick with it. Focusing on your senses will quiet your brain and help you see that you are safe.

A third way to quiet your brain is to **change the channel**.

Changing the channel starts with imagining your brain as a screen, one that is playing **The Worry Show**.

Do you want to watch The Worry Show?

So, just like you would do if you were watching a real show you didn't like, you can change to something else!

You might switch to a brain game, like finding an animal that starts with every letter of the alphabet or counting backwards from 100.

You might change to a song, a long one, and then work hard to remember every word.

Or you can change the channel to a favorite memory, like a time you did something special or succeeded at something that was hard.

Maybe you squeaked out a win in a game of ping pong, or you got to meet your new dog when he was just a pup. Wouldn't it be great to re-watch one of those shows, instead?

If you are going to use a memory, bring to mind as many details as you can. What were you wearing? How did the air smell? What could you hear? How did you feel?

Decide ahead of time how you are going to change the channel on worry.

Draw or write about it here.

A final way to quiet your brain is with **activity**.

Remember we talked about how your body responds to alarms by getting you ready to RUN, FIGHT, or HIDE? Well, running, fighting, and hiding require extra energy. All that extra energy in your body makes it seem like something is wrong. Burning it off helps to quiet your brain, making you feel better inside.

The best way to burn off extra energy is with an activity intense enough to get your heart pounding for at least 10 minutes.

You might:

▶ Run up and down the stairs 20 times.

▶ Hop on your bike for a quick ride around the block.

▶ Roll up a bunch of socks for a fast-paced game of indoor basketball, making fancy hook shots into the nearest laundry hamper.

When your brain alarm is blaring and your worry is at its highest, you might not feel like doing these things. Pick one and do it anyway. You'll be surprised how much it helps.

Draw or write about an active thing you can do to quiet your brain alarm.

All these techniques—breathing, practicing mindfulness, changing the channel, and being active—work best if you practice them ahead of time.

But even with practice, worry might get in the way.

Am I doing it right?

How much longer?

What if the bad thing happens?

I don't think this is helping.

I'm never going to get rid of my worries.

Don't give up.

Keep doing what you were doing, and when worry thoughts bubble up, tell yourself, "That's a worry."

Breathe out long and slow, the way you would breathe if you were blowing on a dandelion. Imagine the worry leaving your brain and floating away.

Practice whichever method you like best for 5 or 10 minutes a day to get your brain used to settling down. Then, when your brain alarm goes off, you'll know exactly what to do.

CHAPTER 5

Using Logic

Understanding how your brain works helps you recognize when you are having an alarm.

Quieting the alarm helps you think more clearly.

Thinking clearly helps with your next step, which is **using logic**.

Using logic means questioning what your worry is telling you instead of immediately believing it. It means staying focused on what is real, and provable, and true. Logic reminds you that really bad things don't happen very often, and that even if something a little bit bad happens, you'll get through it.

Logic helps you make plans, and plans help you feel calmer and less worried.

Using logic starts with putting your worry into words.

What if . . .

I'm afraid that . . .

I'm worried about . . .

Put one of your worries into words.

When you put your worry into words, you might immediately want someone to tell you that it isn't going to happen. This is called looking for **reassurance**.

Reassurance is a funny thing. It can be helpful in new situations, when you have no way of knowing what to expect. But when you are dealing with a worry you've had before and you ask for reassurance, that's like sprinkling water on a tomato plant.

Asking for reassurance over and over again about the very same thing makes worries *grow*.

Using logic takes a little longer, but it's the better thing to do.

Using logic means answering the following three questions:

1. What are the facts?

2. How likely is it?

3. What can I do?

1. What are the facts?

Your brain alarm alerts you when something *seems* scary. But often there is no proof that the scary-seeming thing is real, or likely, or of danger to you. That's why it's important to focus on the facts. Facts are more trustworthy than fears.

Here's an example:

This child is afraid of dogs.

Here are some things they might be thinking.

Circle the facts.
Cross out the fears.

The dog is on a leash.

The dog seems calm.

The leash is tied to a chair.

The dog is going to bite me!

The dog is going to hurt me!

I need to stay back!

The owner is nearby.

No one is getting hurt.

Fears might be loud, but facts are more important. The facts in this example all point to the child being safe.

But there's a wrinkle. Sometimes there's an extra fact, something that is both scary and true.

In the dog example, the extra fact might be this: "Dogs can bite."

Good thing there's another logic question.

yikes!

2. How likely is it?

When you think of a fact that's both scary and true, it's important to sort out how likely it is. Does that thing usually happen, or not? Are there more facts pointing toward the scary possibility, or away from it?

Thinking about how likely (or unlikely) something is means you can say,

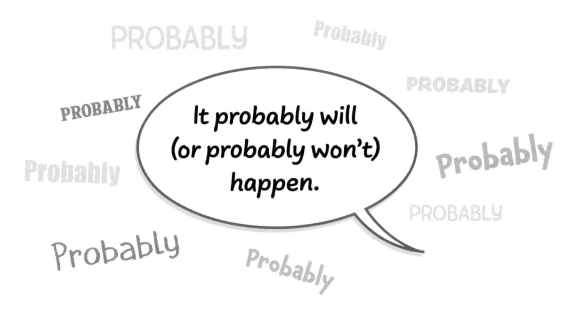

"Probably" might not seem like enough.

You might feel like you need to be totally, absolutely, positively sure. But you can't.

You don't know the future, so you can't be totally, absolutely, positively sure. No one can.

Luckily, you don't have to be *totally* sure. You just need to be sure enough.

Sure enough means that the thing you are worried about is extremely unlikely.

You do things you feel sure enough about all the time. Things that come with a small risk, but not enough to stop you.

► You ride your bike (even though you could fall off).

► You walk into rooms (even though you could stub your toe).

► You try new foods (even though you might not like them).

The list goes on and on.

When worry makes you feel like you need to be 100% sure, remind yourself:

I don't have to be sure. I just need to be sure enough.

Draw or write about something you feel sure enough to do, even though there's a bit of risk.

3. What can I do?

Worry makes you think that the worst possible thing is about to happen. And that there's no way through it.

That simply isn't true. When something goes wrong, it is rarely the **worst thing ever.** It's usually just a bump, and you do get through it.

For example:

Your parent is late for pick-up. ⟹ You and your coach play catch until they arrive.

You answer a question incorrectly. ⟹ The teacher helps you find the right answer, and everyone moves on.

You are at a sleepover, and everyone falls asleep before you. ⟹ You eventually fall asleep.

You can handle bumps. You've done it before, and you can do it again. You are smart, and you are capable, and there will always be people to help you.

So, think about it realistically. If something went wrong, what would happen next? Who would help you? How could you help yourself?

List one of your worries.

Use logic to answer the 3 questions.

1. What are the facts?

2. How likely is it?

3. What can I do?

CHAPTER 6

Talking Back to Worry

Using logic helps you take a step back from worry. But how do you take a step back from something you are thinking about, something you can't even see?

The best way to take a step back is to give your worry a name, and a shape, and a personality.

Imagine your worry like a cloud.

Or a blob.

Or a tomato.

Tomato
Tom

Turn it into a little creature with spikes and googly eyes.

Tomato Tom

Lily Lobster

Worry Worm

Rupert

Alarm-a

Debbie Danger

Miggy

Oh-No

Squirrel

Mister E.

This is your chance to be creative, to imagine Worry however you want.

Draw your Worry here.

Picturing Worry like a little creature lets you take a step back, to think about what it is saying. It also helps you remember that whether this Worry creature is tricky or bossy or silly or mean, it is not in charge of you.

You are the boss of your own life.

The only problem is, Worry doesn't know that.

So, you need to tell it.

Puff out your chest. Put your hands on your hips. Use a strong (but not angry) voice, and tell Worry:

I've got this.

It's my choice, not yours.

Hey, Worry, you are not the boss of me.

No thank you, Worry.

MIGGY

This is called **talking back** to Worry.

The adults in your life might tell you not to talk back. They're right. You shouldn't talk back to parents and teachers and other adults who are trying to help.

But Worry is not an adult, and it isn't being helpful.

So, it is okay to talk back to Worry. Use a voice that is strong and clear. Tell Worry it is not being helpful.

Don't argue with Worry, though. Worry doesn't listen to facts, so arguing is a waste of time.

Instead, say that you don't need Worry's help, and that you aren't going to listen.

"_____"

"_____"

"_____"

Keep in mind that Worry is not a good listener. You might say, "No, thank you, Worry" or "Go away, Worry!" but Worry keeps right on bothering you, and you feel just as afraid as ever.

Don't give up.

Instead, **do something** to show that Worry is not the boss.

CHAPTER 7

Doing the Opposite

Telling Worry isn't enough. You also need to **show** Worry that it is not in charge.

The best way to show Worry is by doing the opposite of what it is telling you to do.

So, quiet your brain.

Use logic.

1. What are the facts?

2. How likely is it?

3. What can I do?

And then gather up your bravery and take a **single step** in the opposite direction of what Worry is saying.

It's okay if the step is small. Even small steps remind you that you don't have to listen to Worry, or believe Worry, or obey Worry.

► Worry tells a child who's afraid of sports mascots to not go to a game.

First step: *Look at pictures of sports mascots online.*

► Worry tells a child who's afraid of bees to not play outside.

First step:_____

► Worry makes a child who frets about not getting picked up on time insist that their parent stay for music lessons.

First step:_____

► Worry stops a child who's afraid of bad guys from going upstairs alone.

First step:_____

► Worry makes a child who's afraid of getting sick feel like they shouldn't eat breakfast.

First step:_____

Of course, after that first step comes a next step, and then another, and another. Each step should be just a little harder than the one before.

Fear: Sports mascots

Step 1: Look at pictures of sports mascots online.
Step 2: Watch videos of sports mascots.
Step 3: Watch a game or show featuring a sports mascot.
Step 4: Go to a game, sitting far from the sports mascot.
Step 5: Go to a game. Sit far from the sports mascot. Zoom in on it with binoculars.
Step 6: Go to a game. Sit closer to the sports mascot.
Step 7: Go to a game. Watch other children interact with the mascot.
Step 8: Go to a game. Greet the mascot.

Write one of your fears.

Fear: _____

Think of a first step.

Step 1: _____

_____

Think of more steps that move you away from what Worry wants.

Step 2: _____

_____

Step 3: _____

_____

Step 4: _____

_____

Step 5: _____

_____

Wahoo! Yay! High five! Good for you!

You are on your way! You are taking back control from Worry.

CHAPTER 8

Spending Less Time With Worry

You have told Worry it's not the boss. You have shown that you mean business by taking steps in the opposite direction of what Worry wants you to do. But Worry might still be getting in the way, taking up too much time.

You can change that. You can spend less time with Worry.

One way to spend less time with Worry is to arrange for a specific **Worry Time.**

Wait a minute! Why would I give Worry **more** time??

Worry Time is 10 or 15 minutes reserved just for Worry. You are going to give Worry that one bit of time because you aren't going to let it interfere at other times. And that one bit of time will happen when you say so, not when Worry demands it.

Worry Time works best for the kinds of worries that come up many times a day and take lots of time once they get started. For worries that happen only at very specific times or about very specific things, skip ahead to the **No More Food for Worry** game.

Start by choosing a time and place for Worry Time. It might be in the family room right after breakfast, or in the kitchen after everyone has cleaned up from dinner. For worries that are big and demanding, you might choose two times. If a parent will be with you for Worry Time, ask them to help you find a time and place that works for everyone. A time you can talk to your parent privately, without interruptions.

When it's your scheduled Worry Time, set a timer for 10 or 15 minutes. Then, talk about whatever worries are on your mind.

It might seem like bedtime is perfect for Worry Time—but it isn't. Worries super-charge your brain, which is the opposite of what your brain needs at bedtime. Bedtime should be your time. A time for reading, cuddling with a parent, and winding down for sleep. Don't give bedtime to Worry.

When it's Worry Time, your parent (or whatever adult you are with) should simply listen. They can tell you that they love you and they have faith in you, but they shouldn't reassure you or try to solve whatever you are worried about. Instead, they can let you know that they hear you, and they understand how hard this is. They can remind you about the logic questions, and help you use your other strategies.

When the timer goes off, Worry Time will be over. If Worry comes knocking at some other time, tell it, "Sorry, Worry, this is my time, not yours."

If you bring up a worry when it isn't Worry Time, your parent can say, "Sorry, Worry, but we're not talking about that right now."

It might feel like they aren't willing to talk to you. But really what they are doing is reminding you to make Worry wait for Worry Time.

Worry isn't going to want to wait. It's used to you **DROPPING EVERYTHING** and **PAYING ATTENTION.**

But here's a little secret: you don't have to drop everything, and you don't have to pay attention.

You can recognize the alarm, breathe, and use your other strategies.

You can tell Worry, "Sorry, pal. You need to wait."

Imagine putting Worry into an imaginary box or cage, or onto a leaf so it can float away.

Draw something to put Worry in or on while you are making it wait for Worry Time.

When you get into the habit of making Worry wait for Worry Time, something interesting will start to happen.

At first, you'll be as bothered by Worry as ever. You'll need to keep stuffing it into that imaginary box or returning it to its cage.

But after a while, when Worry Time rolls around, you will notice that there is less to talk about. Some of the worries you stuck into the cage will have gone away on their own. The little worries that were nagging at you, the ones you used to feel like you needed an answer to right away, those worries will disappear when you stop paying so much attention to them. And then, Worry Time will turn into talking time, or drawing and writing time, a time for you and not for pesky Worry.

There's another way to spend less time with Worry: the **No More Food for Worry** game. It's a funny title to help you remember that Worry "feeds" on time and attention.

When you imagine Worry like a little creature, and you listen to it, and do what it wants you to do, it's like you are handing Worry a bunch of tasty treats.

If, for example, you worry about something happening to your parents and you quiz them about where they are going, you are giving Worry an imaginary slice of pizza. Each question is another slice.

If you worry about getting sick, so you look up signs of illnesses or get a parent to take your temperature, that's a dish of ice cream with chocolate sauce and a cherry.

If you worry about making mistakes, so you avoid things that make you feel unsure, you are giving more and more food to Worry.

Giving Worry tasty treats might feel good right when you do it, but it makes Worry bigger, which means it will take up more time, and more space, and be able to bother you more.

Of course, you haven't been feeding Worry on purpose. You simply didn't know that that's what you were doing. But now you do know, so you can practice feeding Worry less with the **No More Food for Worry Game.** Here's how it works:

No More Food for Worry Game

The set-up:

1. Find 3 index cards or small pieces of paper.

2. Put a question mark on each.

3. Draw some kind of food next to each question mark.

The rules:

1. You get 3 question cards every day.

2. It's your job to keep as many cards as you can.

3. Each time you ask a worry question or go hunting for information to satisfy Worry, your parent will remind you, "That's feeding Worry."

4. If you take the question back, great. You stopped yourself from feeding Worry, so you can keep your cards.

5. If you continue to ask the question or hunt for information, you need to give a card to your parent because you've just fed Worry.

6. If you feed Worry 3 times, you'll be out of cards for the day. Then, if you ask another worry question, your parent can't answer it because you don't have any cards left and answering would be feeding Worry. Instead, they can say something like, "I'm sorry, you're out of cards. No more food for Worry today." They aren't being mean. They are just reminding you to not over-feed Worry because the less food you give it, the smaller Worry will be.

The goal:

Keep as many cards as you can each day. It might take a little while to learn how to say "No" to Worry, but once you do, you will find that you don't need to give it the attention it's demanding. You can talk back to Worry and not let it boss you around, which means— hurray!—you'll be able to keep your cards. If you have one or two cards left at the end of the day, good for you! If you keep all three cards, you earn a prize.

The prize:

Talk to a parent in advance about what your prize might be. Maybe you want points to put toward something fun, like having a friend over or going to a movie. Maybe you want an extra 15 minutes of reading in bed, or to play a game with a parent before dinner. Or you can use a grab bag reward system, which your parent will need to create by writing treats and surprises on small slips of paper. For example:

- Parent will do a chore for you
- Double dessert with dinner
- Family game night
- Pillow fight
- Extra book at bedtime
- Choose parent's outfit for the day

- Outing with a friend
- Paint toenails
- Piggy-back ride upstairs
- Backwards meal
- Trip to bookstore for a new book
- Put a color streak in your hair
- Small toy

When you save all 3 cards in a single day, you can reach into the grab bag, pull out a slip of paper, and—voila!—your reward.

Whether you do **Worry Time**, play the **No More Food for Worry Game**, or use both, keep setting limits on Worry. The less time and attention you give it, the smaller Worry will be.

CHAPTER 9

Staying Healthy and Strong

You are starting to take back control from Worry. Good for you! But Worry can be sneaky, so you need to stay on your toes.

Keep using your strategies, even when you don't feel like it. Even when Worry is small. When it seems like not that big a deal. When you are tired, and there are other things you'd rather be doing.

Using your strategies will get easier over time, but in the beginning, you might find yourself thinking,

Whenever you are doing something hard, you can give yourself a boost by paying attention to the things your brain and body need to stay healthy and strong. Let's talk about those things.

Sleep

As you drift off to sleep, your brain and body get busy doing work they can't do (or can't do as well) when you are awake. For example, while you are asleep, important bits of information get stored in your brain, and unimportant bits get swept away. Your bones grow. Your skin heals. You fight infections.

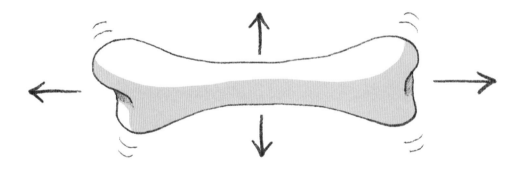

It's a lot of work, which is why getting enough sleep is important. For kids your age, that means between 9 and 12 hours every night.

You'll know you are getting enough sleep when you wake up feeling good, without an alarm. If you need someone to wake you, or you wake up feeling grumpy and tired, you aren't getting enough sleep.

The best way to get more sleep is to move bedtime earlier, just a little bit at a time, even if you don't feel tired. Or you can shorten your bedtime routine. Keep making changes until you reach that sweet spot of waking up on your own, ready for the day.

Nutrition

Food is fuel for humans, but not all food is the same. There are plenty of foods that taste good but don't contain the nutrients we need to be healthy and strong. Filling yourself up with non-nutritious foods might be tempting, but it will make it harder to take back control from Worry.

Your parents can help you find nutrient-rich foods—things like fruits and vegetables, proteins, healthy fats, and whole grains. Nutrient-rich foods are often brightly colored (by nature, not by dyes).

If you aren't already a fan, you can teach yourself to like these foods by trying them again and again.

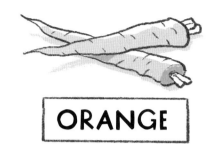

ORANGE

RED

GREEN

Draw or write 5 healthy foods you like and 5 you would be willing to try.

5 Healthy Foods I Like	5 Healthy Foods I Can Try

Drinking enough water is important, too. Water keeps your heart pumping, your joints working, and your brain humming along. It helps with digestion and getting rid of waste (which means your poop will come out more easily).

People who don't drink enough tend to be more tired, crankier, and less able to pay attention.

But there's an easy fix. Drink more! Downing a full glass of water (or other healthy beverage) at every meal is a good place to start.

Exercise

Talking about exercise makes some people groan. They think they'll have to do things that are boring, like jumping jacks, or hard, like push-ups, and get all tired and sweaty. But exercise doesn't have to be unpleasant. In fact, it can be fun. You just need to move your body.

You can play a sport. Jump rope at recess. Race a parent up the stairs.

Fill in the word cloud with your favorite ways of moving your body, and others you'd be willing to try.

SHOOT BASKETS   Skate

Tumble   RUN   Jump

Ride a bike   Dance   HIKE

Getting enough sleep, eating well, and getting exercise every day will keep you healthy and strong. It will also make it easier to use the skills you are learning to take back control from Worry.

CHAPTER 10

You Can Do It!

Whatever you worry about, you are not alone. There are children on your street, in your town, and all around the world learning the strategies you are learning and using them to make Worry a smaller part of their lives.

You are part of a big, diverse community of strong, brave, clever, unique, entirely normal kids. Kids who have decided to take back control from Worry so they can live happier lives.

If you get discouraged, or you forget your strategies, re-read this book. Talk to the grownups who care about you and ask them to help. Make a poster of the skills you have learned and hang it somewhere so you will see it every day. These are your Worry-shrinking strategies, and they will help you re-gain control.

Worry-Shrinking Strategies

1. Recognize you are having an alarm.

2. Quiet the alarm.

3. Use logic.

4. Talk back to Worry.

5. Do the opposite.

6. Spend less time with Worry.

7. Stay healthy and strong.

Keep going, even when it seems hard. You can do it!

It's going to feel so good!

Dawn Huebner, PhD, is a psychologist, parent coach, and the author of numerous self-help books for children, including *What to Do When Your Temper Flares: A Kid's Guide to Overcoming Problems with Anger* and *What to Do When You Dread Your Bed: A Kid's Guide to Overcoming Problems With Sleep.* Specializing in childhood anxiety, Dr. Huebner's work has been translated into 23 languages, touching the lives of millions of children around the world. She lives in Sacramento, CA. Visit her at dawnhuebnerphd.com and on Facebook @DawnHuebnerPhDSelf-HelpforParentsandKids.

Sabine Rothmund studied communication design with a focus on book design and illustration in Mainz and has been working freelance for various publishers for more than 20 years. She lives in Tübingen, Germany.

Magination Press is the children's book imprint of the American Psychological Association. APA works to advance psychology as a science and profession and as a means of promoting health and human welfare. Magination Press books reach young readers and their parents and caregivers to make navigating life's challenges a little easier. It's the combined power of psychology and literature that makes a Magination Press book special. Visit maginationpress.org and @MaginationPress on Facebook, X, Instagram, and Pinterest.